OCEANS ALIVE

Walruses

by Colleen Sexton

BELLWETHER MEDIA · MINNEAPOLIS, MN

BLASTOFF!
2
READERS

Note to Librarians, Teachers, and Parents:

Blastoff! Readers are carefully developed by literacy experts and combine standards-based content with developmentally-appropriate text.

Level 1 provides the most support through repetition of high-frequency words, light text, predictable sentence patterns, and strong visual support.

Level 2 offers early readers a bit more challenge through varied simple sentences, increased text load, and less repetition of high frequency words.

Level 3 advances early-fluent readers toward fluency through increased text and concept load, less reliance on visuals, longer sentences, and more literary language.

Level 4 builds reading stamina by providing more text per page, increased use of punctuation, greater variation in sentence patterns, and increasingly challenging vocabulary.

Level 5 encourages children to move from "learning to read" to "reading to learn" by providing even more text, varied writing styles, and less familiar topics.

Whichever book is right for your reader, Blastoff! Readers are the perfect books to build confidence and encourage a love of reading that will last a lifetime!

This edition first published in 2008 by Bellwether Media.

No part of this publication may be reproduced in whole or in part without written permission of the publisher. For information regarding permission, write to Bellwether Media Inc., Attention: Permissions Department, Post Office Box 1C, Minnetonka, MN 55345-9998.

Library of Congress Cataloging-in-Publication Data
Sexton, Colleen A., 1967–
   Walruses / by Colleen Sexton.
      p. cm. – (Blastoff! readers. Oceans alive)
   Summary: "Simple text and supportive full-color photographs introduce beginning readers to Walruses. Intended for kindergarten through third grade students"–Provided by publisher.
   Includes bibliographical references and index.
   ISBN-13: 978-1-60014-110-2 (hardcover : alk. paper)
   ISBN-10: 1-60014-110-2 (hardcover : alk. paper)
   1. Walrus–Juvenile literature. I. Title.

   QL737.P62S49 2008
   599.79'9–dc22   2007014941

Contents

Walruses live in the **Arctic**.
Winters there are long
and cold.

4

Walruses swim in the ocean
and rest on shore.

Sometimes they catch a
ride on an **ice floe**.

Adult walruses have **tusks**. These long teeth never stop growing.

Walruses hook their tusks onto
the ice and pull themselves
out of the water.

Tusks are strong and hard.
Sometimes the end of a
tusk breaks off.

Walruses have thick skin.

Walruses have **blubber** under their skin to keep them warm.

Sometimes walruses get too
hot. They lie on their backs
to cool off.

flipper

Walruses have four **flippers**.

Walruses use their flippers to walk on land and to swim in the ocean.

Walruses have small eyes.
They cannot see well in
dark water.

Walruses hold their breath to dive. They can stay underwater for 30 minutes!

Walruses mostly eat clams.
They use their thick whiskers
to feel for clams in the mud.

Walruses put their mouths
around clamshells and suck
out the meat.

Walruses swim up for air.
They use their tusks to poke
air holes in the ice.

Walruses eat two meals on most days. They rest when they have finished feeding.

Walruses crowd together to rest. Sometimes they even pile on top of each other!

Glossary

air hole—an opening in the ice where a walrus can come up to breathe

Arctic—the area around the North Pole

blubber—a thick layer of fat under the skin; blubber helps keep a walrus warm in icy waters.

flipper—a flat limb that is shaped like a paddle; flippers help walruses and other sea animals swim.

ice floe—a sheet of floating ice

tusks—a pair of long teeth that are curved and pointed

To Learn More

AT THE LIBRARY
Clarke, Jane. *Tusk Trouble*. New York: Scholastic, 2005.

Kiana, Chris. *Wally the Lost Baby Walrus*. Anchorage, Alaska: Publication Consultants, 1999.

Miller, Connie Colwell. *Walruses*. Mankato, Minn.: Bridgestone Books, 2006.

Young, Carol. *Little Walrus Warning*. Norwalk, Conn.: Soundprints, 1996.

ON THE WEB
Learning more about walruses is as easy as 1, 2, 3.

1. Go to www.factsurfer.com

2. Enter "walruses" into search box.

3. Click the "Surf" button and you will see a list of related web sites.

With factsurfer.com, finding more information is just a click away.

Index

The photographs in this book are reproduced through the courtesy of: James Balog/Getty Images, front cover, pp. 7, 20; Tartan Dragon LTD/Getty Images, pp. 4, 6; Norbert Rosing/Getty Images, pp. 5, 19; Peter Arnold, Inc./Alamy, pp. 8–9; Joseph Van Os/Getty Images, p. 10; blickwinkel/Alamy, p. 11; Jeff Foott/Getty Images, p. 12; Chantal Goupil, p. 13; Frank Greenaway/Getty Images, p. 14; Michael K Nichols/Getty Images, p. 15; Goran Ehime/Sea pics, pp. 16-17; Carlos De Leon/Age fotostock, p. 18; Andrey Stratilatov, p. 19; Joel Sartore/Getty Images, p. 21.